W9-AJP-829

Ofi

Snails
and Other Mollusks

Concept and Product Development: Editorial Options, Inc.
Series Designer: Karen Donica
Book Author: Steven A. Ofinoski

For information on other World Book
products, visit us at our Web site at
http://www.worldbook.com

For information on sales to schools and libraries
in the United States, call 1-800-975-3250.

For information on sales to schools and libraries
in Canada, call 1-800-837-5365.

World Book, Inc.
233 N. Michigan Avenue
Chicago, IL 60601

Library of Congress Cataloging-in-Publication Data

Ofinoski, Steven A.
     Snails and other mollusks.
        p. cm. -- (World Book's animals of the world)
     Summary: Provides information about the physical characteristics, habits, and behavior
     of snails and such related species as clams, oysters, and cuttlefish.
     ISBN 0-7166-1232-1 -- ISBN 0-7166-1223-2 (set)
     1. Snails--Juvenile literature. 2. Mollusks--Juvenile literature. [1. Snails. 2. Mollusks.]
     I. Title. II. Series.

     QL430.4 .O36 2002
     594--dc21   2001046716

Printed in Malaysia

1 2 3 4 5 6 7 8 9 06 05 04 03 02

Picture Acknowledgments: Cover: © Gary Meszaros, Bruce Coleman Inc.; © Fred Bavendam, Minden Pictures; © David B. Fleetham,
Tom Stack & Associates; © A. Flowers & L. Newman, Photo Researchers; © Kjell Sandved, Photo Researchers;

© Ralf Astrom, Bruce Coleman Inc. 9; Fred Bavendam, Minden Pictures 45, 59; © Michael Black, Bruce Coleman Inc. 19; © Jane
Burton, Bruce Coleman Collection 5, 21, 25; © Jane Burton, Bruce Coleman Inc.15; © Scott Camazine, Photo Researchers 57; ©
Douglas Faulkner, Photo Researchers 55; © David B. Fleetham, Tom Stack & Associates 4, 43, 47; © Fletcher & Baylis, Photo
Researchers, 13; © Jeff Foott, Tom Stack & Associates 41; © Valerie Giles, Photo Researchers 9; © David Hosking, Photo Researchers
37; © IFA, Bruce Coleman Inc. 7; © Breck P. Kent, Animals Animals 35; © A. Flowers & L. Newman, Photo Researchers 53; © Zig
Leszczynski, Animals Animals 33; © Gary Meszaros, Bruce Coleman Inc. 3; © M. Timothy O'Keefe, Bruce Coleman Inc. 23; © Ed
Robinson, Tom Stack & Associates 61; © Kjell Sandved, Photo Researchers 29; © Mike Severns, Tom Stack & Associates 11, 49;
© M. H. Sharp, Photo Researchers 4, 27; © Tom Stack & Associates, 9; © Kim Taylor, Bruce Coleman Collection 9; © George Whiteley,
Photo Researchers 31; © Dr. Paul A. Zahl, Photo Researchers 39.

Illustrations: WORLD BOOK illustration by Michael DiGiorgio 17, 51; WORLD BOOK illustration by Kersti Mack 62.

World Book's Animals of the World

Snails
and Other Mollusks

How did I end up here?

World Book, Inc.
A Scott Fetzer Company
Chicago

Contents

Wanna hug?

How do I keep a clam from clamming up?

Do I put my eggs
in a basket?

What Are Mollusks?

Mollusks are soft-bodied animals. Snails are mollusks. Clams, octopuses, and squids are mollusks, too. Mollusks are invertebrates *(ihn VUR tuh brihts),* or animals without backbones. In fact, mollusks have no bones at all.

Most mollusks have hard shells. The shells protect their soft bodies. Some mollusks, such as snails, have spiral shells. Others, such as clams and oysters, have hinged shells. Some mollusks, such as squids, have internal shells.

There are about 50,000 species, or kinds, of mollusks alive today. In fact, scientists discover new species each year. And scientists know from studying fossils that thousands more mollusks lived long ago.

Snail

Where in the World Do Mollusks Live?

Mollusks live in many places throughout the world. Most mollusks live in bodies of water, such as oceans, rivers, and ponds. Mollusks also live on land in places where they can keep their bodies moist.

Most land snails live in damp places, such as shady forests and wetlands. But some snails even find enough water to survive in deserts. Oysters, clams, and scallops live in the shallow, coastal waters of oceans. Many octopuses and squids make their home in the ocean deep.

Ocean

Pond

Forest

Coast

How Does a Snail Make Its Shell?

Nearly all mollusks have shells. Most mollusks also have organs called mantles. The mantle is thin and a bit like skin. In a snail, it lines the shell. A snail, like most other mollusks, uses its mantle to make its shell.

To make a shell, the mantle releases a liquid made up of shell materials. Gradually the liquid hardens and forms the shell. Over time, the mantle releases more of this liquid. This in turn adds to the size of the shell.

Snail shells come in many different shapes and sizes. Most snails have spiraled shells, like this tree snail. Some sea snails have shells that coil into cones. Other snails even have shells that are shaped like macaroni!

Tree snail

How Does a Snail Get Around?

A snail gets around on its foot. But it's not the kind of foot you might be thinking of. A snail's foot is actually a long, muscular organ that spreads out under the snail's body.

A land snail moves forward by making a rippling motion with its foot. As it moves, the snail releases a slippery slime. The slime coats the ground under the snail. This helps the snail move along a little more easily. If you watch a snail cross a yard, you can see the trail of slime it leaves behind.

Slime or no slime, snails are very slow animals. It would take a snail moving at top speed more than a day to move from one end of an American football field to the other!

Snail crawling

When Does a Snail Crawl into Its Shell?

A snail crawls into its shell when it senses that an enemy is nearby. Remember, a snail is very slow. So it usually can't escape from an enemy, such as a snake, a frog, or a bird. That's where the shell comes in. It protects the snail from enemy attack.

Once safely curled up inside, snails can close off their shells. Different kinds of snails do this in different ways. One kind moves the hard part of its foot over the shell's opening. Another kind spreads a layer of hardened slime over the opening. With the shell opening sealed off, the snail is safe from most attacks. It can stay sealed up like this for days or even weeks.

During long periods of heat or cold, snails may also curl up in their shell to stay moist. They hardly move and need little food or water. This state is similar to how a bear hibernates. When snails go though this process, it's called estivation *(EHS tuh VAY shuhn).*

Snail curled up in shell

Do Snails Have Eyes?

Snails do have eyes, but not all snails have eyes in the same spot on their bodies. A land snail has two pairs of tentacles that stick out from its head. On the tip of the two longer tentacles are its eyes. A land snail can move its tentacles up and down and from side to side to help it get the best view. But a sea snail's eyes are located at the base of its tentacles. And they always stay in one place.

Not only do land and sea snails see things differently, but they breathe differently, too. A land snail breathes using its lung. Its lung is located in a fold in the mantle called the *mantle cavity*.

Sea snails breathe through gills. Like fish, they use their gills to get oxygen from the water. A sea snail's gills are located in its mantle cavity.

Some freshwater snails have gills, too. Others have lungs, just like land snails. When they need to breathe air, they must come to the surface.

Diagrams of Two Snails

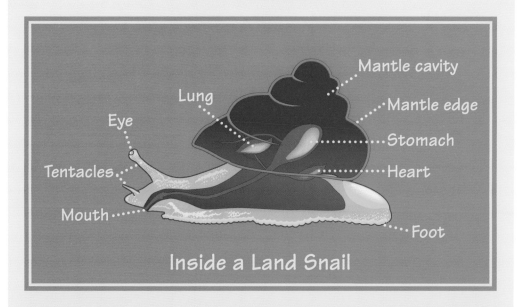

Inside a Land Snail

Mantle cavity
Lung
Eye
Mantle edge
Tentacles
Stomach
Heart
Mouth
Foot

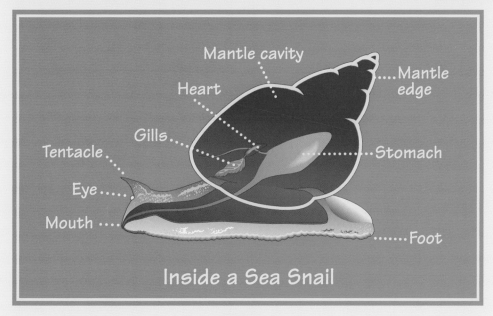

Inside a Sea Snail

Mantle cavity
Heart
Mantle edge
Gills
Tentacle
Stomach
Eye
Mouth
Foot

What Do Snails Eat?

Snails eat many types of foods. Land snails mostly eat dying plants. They also eat fruits, living plants, and sometimes bark, too. Freshwater snails eat algae *(AL jee)* and the remains of dead animals and plants. Sea snails mostly feed on algae. Some also eat other small animals.

How do snails eat? Snails have teeth, but they are not like any teeth you've ever seen. Nearly all snails have radulas *(RAJ u luhz)*. Radulas are hard, ribbonlike organs that look like tongues. Radulas contain rows of tiny teeth. Some snails have just a few teeth while others have thousands. As these teeth wear away over time, they are replaced by new ones.

Snails don't chew their food. Instead, they use their radulas to grind, grate, and tear it.

Snail eating

Does a Land Snail Lay Eggs?

Yes, like most other snails, a land snail lays eggs. Most land snail eggs are very small. They are about the same size and shape as this: **O**. Over a few days, a land snail may lay around 100 eggs. But most of these eggs are eaten by predators.

A land snail lays its eggs in a small hole it digs in the soil. It covers the eggs with a mixture of dirt and slime. After about two to four weeks, the eggs hatch. The tiny newborn snails have very big appetites. They eat whatever is nearby—including what's left of their eggshell. Some newborn snails will even eat other unhatched eggs!

Life is not easy for young snails. Very few snails live to be a year old. Most are killed by predators such as birds, beetles, and fish. Young snails that survive the tough first year still have some growing to do. They don't become adults until they are about 2 years old.

Land snail laying eggs

Where Do Sea Snails Lay Their Eggs?

Many sea snails, like the queen conch pictured here, lay their eggs on the floors of tropical oceans where they live. Some sea snails lay thousands of eggs over a few days. In fact, the queen conch can lay over 500,000 eggs at one time! But, like land snail eggs, most of these eggs are eaten by predators.

However, many queen conch eggs do hatch, and some of these young snails live long enough to become adults. An adult queen conch is one of the largest snails. It may grow a shell that is 1 foot (30 centimeters) long.

Queen conch

What Are Periwinkles?

Periwinkles are a group of sea snails. There are many kinds of periwinkles, including the flat periwinkle, the checkered periwinkle, the marsh periwinkle, and even the zebra periwinkle. The common periwinkle lives along the shores of northern Europe and the Atlantic coast of North America. The average periwinkle is about 1 inch (25 millimeters) long and 3/4 of an inch (19 millimeters) wide.

Different kinds of periwinkles live on different parts of the shore. Some periwinkles live near the high-tide line. Others make their homes near the low-tide line. At low tide, when the water goes out, some periwinkles coil up inside their shells to stay moist. This also keeps them safe from predators. When the water returns at high tide, the periwinkles come out from their shells to graze on algae and tiny plants.

Flat periwinkles

Which Snails Eat Other Mollusks?

Whelks are large sea snails with hard, spiral shells. The knobbed whelk of the Atlantic coast, pictured here, can grow 8 inches (20 centimeters) long. This whelk, like many other whelks, often eats other mollusks.

A whelk's main diet is clams. And whelks are experts at opening up a clam's shell. First, a whelk grasps the clam in its foot. Next, it rubs its shell on the clam until the clam's shell chips or cracks. Then the whelk slowly pries the clam apart until the clam's body is exposed. Whelks eat the remains of dead animals, too.

Knobbed whelk

Which Snails Don't Have Shells?

Slugs look like snails without shells, and that's exactly what they are. In fact, most slugs go through life without shells. This might seem dangerous for animals that move so slowly. But slugs have some ways to stay safe that really work.

Many land and sea slugs have colors that blend in with their surroundings. This makes it hard for predators to see them. Other slugs, like this nudibranch *(NOO duh brangk)*, have bright colors that warn predators to stay away. Their brilliant colors let enemies know that they don't taste good.

Sea slugs have other tricks to escape their enemies, too. Some can simply swim away. Others release a foul smell that usually keeps an enemy from getting too close.

Nudibranch

Why Does a Clam Clam Up?

Most snails have one-piece shells. But all clams have shells made up of two parts called valves. That's why clams and their relatives are called bivalves. Like snail shells, clam shells are good protection.

Have you ever opened a hinged jewelry box? A clam's shell opens and closes in much the same way. The two valves are just about the same size and shape. They are connected on one side by a strong ligament and muscles. A clam opens its shell when it is safe. But at the first sign of danger, it clams right up.

Like a snail, a clam has a foot. A clam uses its foot to burrow into the sand or mud on the floor of freshwater lakes or oceans.

Two common families of clams are soft-shelled clams and hard-shelled clams. Hard-shelled clams have thick shells that are shaped a bit like hearts. Soft-shelled clams have thinner and longer shells.

Hard-shelled clam

How Does a Clam Eat?

Each clam has two siphons *(SY fuhnz)*. These are round openings in the clam's mantle cavity where water comes in and goes out. The water contains bits of food that the clam gathers and then eats.

Here is how the process works. The water enters the clam's body through one siphon. From there it flows into the clam's gills. The gills capture oxygen from the water, but they also trap food. In the clam's gills are tiny hairs called cilia *(SIHL ee uh)*. The cilia catch the particles of food drifting in the water and bring it to the clam's mouth. The water then flows out of the clam through the other siphon.

A clam doesn't have to work very hard for its meals. Its main food is plankton, which is a mass of very small water organisms. Water currents carry plankton right to the clam.

Soft-shelled clam

How Can You Tell an Oyster's Age?

You can tell an oyster's age by reading the rings on its shell. Each ring takes about one year to grow. Biologists can "read" the rings to tell how old an oyster is.

As long as its body grows, the oyster's shell continues to grow, too. A young oyster grows at a rate of about 1 inch (2.5 centimeters) per year. Eastern oysters, like the one you see here, grow to 10 inches (25 centimeters) in length.

Eastern oyster

How Does an Oyster Make a Pearl?

A beautiful pearl actually starts out as a grain of sand or dirt. Water carries the grain into an oyster's mantle, where it settles. The rough grain can really disturb the oyster's soft body. So the oyster uses its mantle to produce a soft substance that covers the grain. Over time, the substance hardens. Eventually, the covering over the grain grows in size and becomes a smooth pearl.

Not all oysters make perfect pearls. Chances are that any pearls you've seen were made by pearl oysters. True oysters, the kind people eat, sometimes make pearls, too. But their pearls look more like hard gray peas. Not many people want to wear necklaces made of these!

Pearl oyster

Which Bivalve Can Swim All on Its Own?

The scallop, unlike most other bivalves, can propel itself across the ocean floor. The scallop has a special muscle that lies near the center of its body. It uses this muscle to open and close its shell quickly. This forces water out of its mantle cavity, causing the scallop to move as much as 3 feet (91 centimeters).

A scallop doesn't move very often. But when it does, it's usually because a sea star or other predator is near. Sometimes, a scallop spurts water out of its shell to make a resting hole in the sandy ocean floor.

Scallop swimming

Which Mollusks Have Eight-Piece Shells?

A univalve has one valve. A bivalve has two. But some mollusks have eight valves. They are called chitons *(KY tuhnz)*. A chiton's eight valves, or plates, overlap one another. The plates are held together by a piece of tough, leathery flesh called a girdle.

A chiton has a very long and wide foot. With its long foot, a chiton can cling to coastal rocks. In fact, a chiton spends most of its life clinging to these rocks. There it feeds on algae and other tiny organisms in the seawater.

If a strong wave or a predator causes the chiton to lose its grip, it will roll itself into a ball for defense—just like an armadillo.

Chiton

How Many Arms Does an Octopus Have?

An octopus doesn't have a shell. But it does have eight long and muscular arms. Some octopuses, such as the day octopus, have arms up to seven times the length of their bodies. Imagine having arms like that!

Each of an octopus's arms has a row of suckers. These suckers help the octopus cling to almost anything. An octopus uses its powerful arms to capture and tear apart prey such as crabs, clams, and snails. It can also use its arms to move along the ocean floor.

Day octopus

Why Does an Octopus Squirt Ink?

An octopus sometimes squirts a unique substance called ink into the water. It does this when it needs to defend itself from predators such as seals, whales, and sharks.

The Pacific giant octopus, like many other kinds of octopus, may squirt ink to make the water dark. That way, a predator can't see the octopus escape. At other times, the inky cloud serves as a decoy. The cloud actually looks like the octopus itself. As the predator attacks the decoy, the real octopus makes its getaway!

Squirting ink isn't the only way an octopus can escape its enemy, though. It can swim quickly away if it has to. It can also change its color. This often confuses the predator and gives the octopus time to flee. Other times, the octopus changes its color to blend in with its surroundings. Then the octopus may not be seen at all.

Pacific giant octopus
squirting ink

Which Octopus Is the Deadliest?

The blue-ringed octopus lives off the southern Australian coast. This tiny octopus is only 1 1/2 to 2 1/2 inches (4 to 6 centimeters) in diameter. But don't let its small size fool you. This octopus is the most deadly octopus of all.

Instead of making ink, the blue-ringed octopus makes venom in its saliva. When the blue-ringed octopus bites its victim, it leaves saliva on the wound. The venom in the saliva causes the area around the wound to go numb. Soon, the venom causes the octopus's victim to stop breathing. The venom is so deadly that it can kill even a human.

This octopus feeds mostly on crabs that live in shallow waters. When it is threatened, its blue rings glow. This warning is usually all that it takes to scare most predators away!

Blue-ringed octopus

Who Wear Their Shells on the Inside?

Squids do! Squids are mollusks that are closely related to octopuses. Squids have horny internal shells, also called *pens*. Pens protect squids in much the same way as the external shells of other mollusks protect them.

Squids have eight arms, just as octopuses do. But they also have two tentacles that extend from their heads. Both the arms and the tentacles have rows of sucking disks that are used to hold such prey as fish, crabs, and other squid.

Of all mollusks, squids are the best swimmers. To swim, squids fill part of their bodies with water. Then they force the water through a tube. This allows the squids to shoot through the water in quick bursts. That's why squids are also called *sea arrows*.

Squid

Which Mollusks Are Giants?

Giant squids are true giants. These monsters of the deep can grow to a length of 60 feet (18 meters). That's about twice the length of a school bus! Not surprisingly, giant squids are the largest invertebrates on Earth.

It's easy to see why giant squids have long been the stuff of legends. Their huge, parrotlike beaks are so strong that they can crush bone. Each sucker on a giant squid's eight arms may be as big as a dinner plate. Imagine swimming next to one of these mollusks!

Giant squids live about 3,000 feet (900 meters) down in the ocean depths. That's so deep that scientists don't know much about how they live. As a matter of fact, no one has ever seen a living giant squid.

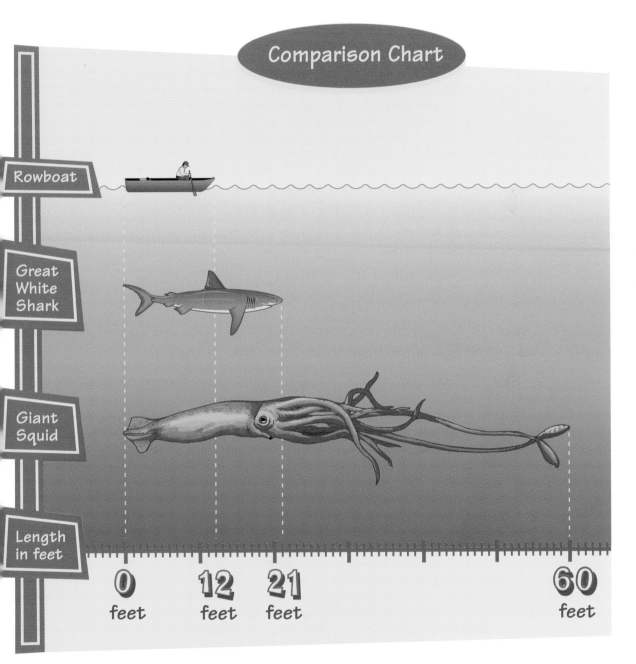

Comparison Chart

Rowboat

Great White Shark

Giant Squid

Length in feet

0 feet

12 feet

21 feet

60 feet

Are Cuttlefish Really Fish?

No, cuttlefish are actually small mollusks. They are related to squids and octopuses. Like a squid, a cuttlefish has an internal shell.

Cuttlefish have oval bodies that can come in all sorts of colors, such as white, brown, orange, red, and green. Some cuttlefish even change color, depending on the way sunlight hits their bodies.

Like a squid and an octopus, a cuttlefish has eight arms. A cuttlefish also has two long tentacles. But unlike a squid, a cuttlefish can tuck its tentacles into pockets above its eyes. That's some trick!

Orange cuttlefish

Which Mollusks Are Living Fossils?

There are six species of nautilus *(NAH tuh luhs)* alive today. These mollusks have been around for millions of years. During that time, they have not changed at all. Many more kinds of nautilus lived long ago. Scientists have recorded over 2,000 different fossil forms of these mollusks.

A nautilus has a cone-shaped head ringed by about 90 short tentacles. The tentacles stretch out to catch small crabs, shrimp, and algae. The body of a full-grown nautilus is about the size of an adult human's fist.

These ancient mollusks live in water depths of 20 to 1,000 feet (6 to 300 meters) in the South Pacific and Indian oceans. Nautiluses are also related to squids and octopuses.

Nautilus

How Many Chambers Can a Nautilus Make?

An average nautilus can make about 30 chambers during its life. A chamber is a section of a nautilus's shell. It's where the nautilus lives within its shell. As the nautilus grows, it makes a newer and slightly larger chamber to live in. Over time, the shell gradually takes the form of a spiral.

Even with its external shell, the nautilus can swim well. As the nautilus grows older, it moves into the outermost chamber. From there it fills the older inner chambers with a gas. This helps the shell to float, which in turn enables the nautilus to swim.

Cutaway of a
Nautilus shell

What Are Argonauts?

Argonauts *(AHR guh nawts)* are mollusks that are closely related to octopuses. Female argonauts can grow to more than 18 inches (46 centimeters) in length. Also, the females produce paper-thin shells in which they live and store eggs.

Because of these paper-thin shells, argonauts are sometimes called paper nautiluses. This includes the males, even though they have no shells. Males are also much smaller than females. They grow to only about 1 inch (2.5 centimeters) long.

Argonauts live near the surface of warm seas, where they feed on small fish. The ancient Greeks believed argonauts sailed on the water by using two of their arms as sails. Because of this, they named the mollusk after the sailors of the ship *Argo.* They were the sailors who went to look for the Golden Fleece with Jason in the famous Greek myth.

Female argonaut

Are Mollusks in Danger?

Some mollusks are in danger. Pollution threatens many bivalves, such as the giant clam and many kinds of oysters. Also people overharvest these bivalves for food. People kill large numbers of bivalves and snails for their unique shells. Other mollusks, such as squids, are often caught accidentally in fishing nets, where they quickly die.

Today, laws protect many endangered mollusks. Other mollusks may benefit from changes in human activities. For example, people now create oyster beds, where they place young oysters. After these oysters grow, oyster farmers collect them for food. Harvesting oysters grown in beds allows wild populations to remain untouched. As long as people continue efforts like these, most mollusks will be here for a long time to come.

Giant clam

Mollusk Fun Facts

→ The giant African snail grows to a length of 6 inches (15 centimeters).

→ Female oysters can produce as many as 500 million eggs in a year.

→ Land snails, also known as escargot *(ehs kahr GOH)*, are eaten by many people around the world.

→ Some squids can swim up to 25 miles (40 kilometers) per hour.

→ If an octopus loses one of its eight arms, it grows a new one in its place.

→ An octopus has three hearts.

Glossary

algae A simple organism that lives in water or moist soil.

bivalve A mollusk with a shell made up of two parts.

cilia Tiny hairs in the gills of some sea mollusks.

estivation A long period when snails stay curled up inside their shells.

gill A part of a mollusk's body that is used to breathe in water.

hibernation A sleeplike state.

ink A cloudy substance that octopuses sometimes squirt into the water.

invertebrate An animal without a backbone.

mantle A sheet of tissue that lines a mollusk's shell.

mantle cavity A space within a mollusk's mantle that contains its gills or lung.

pen A horny internal shell.

plankton Tiny organisms that drift near the surface in bodies of water.

radula A hard, ribbonlike organ that snails use to eat their food.

siphon A round opening in some water mollusks where water comes in and goes out.

species A group of the same kind of animals.

sucker A disk on an arm or tentacle that is used to grasp with.

tentacle A long, flexible organ on some mollusks that is used to grasp food and to feel with.

valve One of the separate parts of a mollusk shell.

venom A poison made by some kinds of animals.

Index

(**Boldface** indicates a photo or illustration.)

For more information about mollusks, try these resources:

Eyewitness: Shells, by Alex Arthur, Dorling Kindersley, 2000

The Octopus: Phantom of the Sea, by Mary M. Cerullo, Cobblehill Books, 1997

Snails and Slugs (Nature Up-Close), by Elaine Pasco, Blackbirch Press, 1998

http://www.cyhaus.com/marine/mollusk.htm

http://seawifs.gsfc.nasa.gov/squid.html

http://www.mbayaq.org/efc/efc_fo/fo_octopus.asp

Mollusk Classification

Scientists classify animals by placing them into groups. The animal kingdom is a group that contains all the world's animals. Phylum, class, order, and family are smaller groups. Each phylum contains many classes. A class contains orders, an order contains families, and a family contains individual species. Each species also has its own scientific name. Here is how the animals in this book fit in to this system.

Mollusks (Phylum Mollusca)

Chitons (Class Polyplacophora)

Clams, oysters, scallops, and their relatives (Class Bivalvia)

Hard-shelled clams and their relatives (Order Veneroida)

Hard-shelled clams (Family Veneridae)

Pearl oysters and their relatives (Order Pterioida)

Pearl oysters (Family Pteriidae)

Scallops, true oysters and their relatives (Order Ostreoidae)

Scallops (Family Pectinidae)

True oysters (Family Ostreidae)

Soft-shelled clams and their relatives (Order Myoida)

Soft-shelled clams (Family Myidae)

Slugs and snails (Class Gastropoda)

Land snails and their relatives (Order Stylommatophora)

Conches, periwinkles, whelks and their relatives (Order Neotaenioglossa)

Periwinkles (Family Littorinidae)
Checkered periwinkle. . . . . *Littorina scutulata*
Common periwinkle . . . . *Littorina littorea*
Flat periwinkle . . . . *Littorina obtusata*
Marsh periwinkle. . . . . *Littoraria irrorata*
Zebra periwinkle . . . . *Nodilittorina ziczac*

Conches (Family Strombidae)
Queen conch. . . . . *Strombus gigas*

Whelks (Families Buccinidae and Melongenidae)
Knobbed whelk . . . . *Busycon carica*

Squids, octopuses, and their relatives (Class Cephalopoda)

Cuttlefish and their relatives (Order Sepioidea)

Cuttlefish (Family Sepiidae)

Nautiluses (Order Nautilida)

Nautiluses (Family Nautilidae)

Octopuses and their relatives (Order Octopoda)

Argonauts (Family Argonautidae)

Octopuses (Family Octopodidae)
Blue-ringed octopuses . . . . *Hapalochlaena sp.*
Day octopus . . . . *Octopus cyaneus*
Pacific giant octopus. . . . . *Octopus dofleini*

Squids (Order Teuthoidea)

Giant squids (Family Architeuthidae)
Atlantic giant squid . . . . *Architeuthis dux*